RANJOT SINGH CHAHAL

How to Spend Time Well

A Practical Guide to Productivity That Enhances Your Efficiency and Fulfillment

First published by Rana Books 2024

Copyright © 2024 by Ranjot Singh Chahal

All rights reserved. No part of this publication may be reproduced, stored or transmitted in any form or by any means, electronic, mechanical, photocopying, recording, scanning, or otherwise without written permission from the publisher. It is illegal to copy this book, post it to a website, or distribute it by any other means without permission.

First edition

Contents

1. The Importance of Time Management — 1
2. Assessing Your Current Time Management Skills — 10
3. Setting Goals and Priorities — 19
4. Creating a Time Management Plan — 25
5. Overcoming Procrastination — 35
6. Delegating and Outsourcing Tasks — 43
7. Time Management Tools and Techniques — 51
8. Managing Distractions and Interruptions — 58
9. Maintaining Work-Life Balance — 67
10. Improving Efficiency and Productivity — 76
11. Time Management for Specific Situations — 81
12. Monitoring and Adjusting Your Time Management System — 87

1

The Importance of Time Management

Time management is a crucial skill that affects every aspect of our lives, from personal well-being to professional success. It involves planning and organizing how much time you spend on specific activities to effectively achieve your goals. Effective time management allows individuals to be more productive, reduce stress, and create a better work-life balance. In this essay, we will explore the importance of time management in detail, discussing its benefits, strategies, and real-life examples.

Importance of Time Management

1. Enhanced Productivity

Time management is essential for enhancing productivity. By planning and organizing tasks effectively, individuals can optimize their efforts to achieve more in less time. When you manage your time well, you can prioritize important tasks, allocate sufficient time for each activity, and reduce distractions that may hinder your progress. This results in higher productivity levels and improved performance.

For example, a student who effectively manages their time can allocate specific study hours for each subject, complete assignments on time, and adequately prepare for exams. As a result, they are likely to perform better academically compared to a student who procrastinates and fails to manage their time effectively.

2. Reduced Stress

Poor time management often leads to increased stress levels. When individuals struggle to meet deadlines, juggle multiple tasks simultaneously, or feel overwhelmed by their workload, they experience heightened stress and anxiety. However, by managing time efficiently, individuals can alleviate stress by breaking tasks into manageable chunks, setting realistic goals, and ensuring sufficient time for relaxation and self-care.

For instance, a professional who effectively schedules meetings, sets aside time for focused work, and avoids last-minute rushes is less likely to experience work-related stress compared to someone who constantly feels overwhelmed by their workload due to poor time management.

3. Improved Decision-Making

Good time management skills enhance decision-making abilities. When you manage your time effectively, you have a clearer understanding of your goals, priorities, and deadlines. This clarity enables you to make informed decisions about how to allocate your time and resources wisely. By making conscious choices about where to invest your time, you can pursue activities that align with your objectives and values.

For example, a business owner who prioritizes time management can make strategic decisions about resource allocation, project timelines, and team management based on a careful assessment of available time and priorities. This leads to more effective decision-making and better outcomes for the business.

4. Work-Life Balance

Time management plays a critical role in achieving work-life balance. Individuals who effectively manage their time can allocate sufficient hours to work, family, personal development, and leisure activities. By setting boundaries and managing time effectively, they prevent work from encroaching on their personal life, leading to a healthier and more fulfilling lifestyle.

For instance, a professional who practices good time management can leave work on time, spend quality time with family and friends, pursue hobbies and interests, and prioritize self-care activities. This balance between work and personal life contributes to overall well-being and satisfaction.

5. Increased Efficiency

Efficient time management enhances overall efficiency. When you plan and structure your tasks effectively, you can eliminate time-wasting activities, minimize distractions, and focus on high-priority tasks. By working on tasks systematically and avoiding procrastination, you can complete tasks more quickly and with higher quality, leading to increased efficiency in your daily activities.

For example, a project manager who creates a detailed schedule, delegates tasks efficiently, and monitors progress regularly can ensure that the project progresses smoothly and meets its deadlines. This level of efficiency is crucial for achieving project success and meeting stakeholder expectations.

Strategies for Effective Time Management

1. Set SMART Goals

Setting Specific, Measurable, Achievable, Relevant, and Time-bound (SMART) goals is essential for effective time management. By defining clear objectives and deadlines, you can create a roadmap for your tasks and prioritize your activities accordingly. SMART goals help you stay focused, motivated, and accountable for your time management efforts.

For example, if a student sets a SMART goal of completing a research paper by a specific deadline, they are more likely to break down the task into smaller milestones, allocate time for research, writing, and editing, and monitor their progress to ensure timely completion.

2. Prioritize Tasks

Prioritizing tasks based on their importance and urgency is key to effective time management. By categorizing tasks as high, medium, or low priority, you can focus on completing critical tasks first and then move on to less urgent activities. This ensures that important deadlines are met, and critical objectives are achieved in a timely manner.

For instance, a professional prioritizes tasks by creating a daily to-do list, identifying the most important tasks that must be completed that day, and allocating time and resources accordingly. This approach helps them tackle high-priority items efficiently before addressing less urgent matters.

3. Create a Schedule

Creating a daily, weekly, or monthly schedule helps you allocate time for specific activities, tasks, and responsibilities. By structuring your day and mapping out your commitments, you can ensure that you make the most of your time and avoid last-minute rushes or missed deadlines. A well-planned schedule provides a framework for managing your time effectively.

For example, an entrepreneur creates a weekly schedule that includes time blocks for meetings, client calls, business development activities, and personal time. By following this schedule, they can balance work responsibilities with personal commitments and avoid overloading their calendar.

4. Use Time Management Tools

Utilizing time management tools and techniques can enhance your productivity and efficiency. From digital apps and software to traditional planners and calendars, there are various tools available to help you organize tasks, set reminders, track progress, and manage your time effectively. By leveraging these tools, you can streamline your workflow and stay organized.

For instance, a freelancer uses a project management tool to track deadlines, collaborate with clients, and monitor project progress. This tool allows them to centralize all project information, set reminders for key milestones, and ensure timely delivery of their work.

5. Learn to Delegate

Delegating tasks to others is an important aspect of time management. By entrusting certain responsibilities to team members or outsourcing tasks that are not within your expertise, you can free up time for more critical activities that align with your strengths and priorities. Delegation helps you focus on high-impact tasks and improves overall efficiency.

For example, a manager delegates administrative tasks to an assistant, allowing them to concentrate on strategic decision-making, client interactions, and project oversight. By assigning non-core activities to others, the manager can optimize their time and leverage their skills effectively.

6. Practice Time Blocking

Time blocking involves setting aside dedicated blocks of time for specific tasks or activities. By allocating focused time periods for individual tasks or projects, you can reduce interruptions, maintain concentration, and increase productivity. Time blocking helps you create a structured workday and ensure that you allocate sufficient time for essential activities.

For instance, a writer practices time blocking by dedicating the mornings to writing projects, the afternoons to research and editing, and the evenings to self-development activities. This approach allows them to allocate focused time for each task and optimize their output throughout the day.

7. Limit Multitasking

While multitasking may seem like a way to accomplish more in less time, it often leads to decreased productivity and increased errors. By focusing on one task at a time and completing it before moving on to the next, you can increase efficiency, improve quality, and reduce the likelihood of errors. Limiting multitasking allows you to devote full attention to each task and produce better results.

For example, a professional avoids multitasking during client calls by focusing on active listening, taking notes, and engaging with the client effectively. By concentrating on one task at a time, they can provide better service, avoid misunderstandings, and build stronger client relationships.

Real-Life Examples of Time Management

1. Elon Musk

Elon Musk, the CEO of Tesla and SpaceX, is known for his rigorous approach to time management. Despite leading multiple companies simultaneously and overseeing ambitious projects, Musk prioritizes efficient time allocation to maximize productivity. He segments his day into five-minute blocks, schedules meetings in brief time slots, and sets aggressive timelines for project deliverables. Musk's disciplined approach to time management allows him to juggle various responsibilities effectively and drive innovation in the aerospace and automotive industries.

2. Serena Williams

Serena Williams, one of the most successful tennis players in history, exemplifies effective time management in sports. Williams maintains a strict training schedule, balancing practice sessions, workout routines, and tournament preparation to stay at the top of her game. By dedicating focused hours to physical training, mental conditioning, and skill development, Williams maximizes her performance on the tennis court. Her commitment to time management enables her to achieve consistent success in competitive tennis and remain a dominant figure in the sport.

3. Warren Buffett

Warren Buffett, the renowned investor and CEO of Berkshire Hathaway, emphasizes the importance of time management in achieving long-term financial success. Buffett attributes his investment prowess to disciplined decision-making, patience, and strategic time allocation. By conducting thorough research, focusing on high-quality investments, and avoiding impulsive decisions, Buffett optimizes his time spent analyzing market opportunities and managing his investment portfolio. His prudent approach to time management has enabled him to build substantial wealth and become one of the most successful investors in history.

Conclusion

In conclusion, time management is a fundamental skill that influences productivity, stress levels, decision-making, work-life balance, and overall efficiency. By prioritizing tasks, setting goals, creating schedules, using time management tools, learning to delegate, and practicing effective techniques such as time blocking, individuals can optimize their time and achieve better outcomes in various aspects of their lives. Real-life examples of successful individuals like Elon Musk, Serena Williams, and Warren Buffett demonstrate the impact of effective time management on professional success and personal achievement. By recognizing the importance of time management and implementing strategies to improve how we allocate our time, we can enhance our performance, reduce stress, and lead more fulfilling lives. Mastering time management is not just about managing schedules and deadlines—it is about making conscious choices that align with our goals, values, and priorities to achieve success and well-being in the long run.

2

Assessing Your Current Time Management Skills

Assessing one's current time management skills is a crucial step towards improving productivity and efficiency. It involves evaluating how effectively you allocate and utilize your time to achieve your goals and tasks. Understanding your strengths and weaknesses in managing time allows you to make necessary adjustments and adopt better strategies for maximizing productivity. Through self-assessment, feedback from others, and various tools and techniques, you can gain valuable insights into your time management habits and identify areas for improvement.

Why Assess Time Management Skills?

Effective time management is essential for personal and professional success. By assessing your time management skills, you can:

1. Identify inefficiencies: Assessing your time management

skills helps you recognize where time is being wasted or underutilized.

2. Boost productivity: Understanding how you use your time allows you to make targeted improvements to enhance productivity.

3. Reduce stress: Improved time management reduces the pressure of deadlines and helps in achieving a better work-life balance.

4. Enhance goal achievement: Efficient time management enables you to focus on tasks that align with your goals and priorities.

5. Improve decision-making: By assessing your time management skills, you can make informed decisions about task prioritization and resource allocation.

Methods for Assessing Time Management Skills

1. Self-Reflection: Reflecting on your daily routines, work habits, and time allocation helps in understanding how you currently manage your time. Ask yourself questions like:
    - How do I prioritize tasks?
    - What time-wasting habits do I have?
    - Do I set realistic goals and deadlines?
    - How well do I estimate task durations?

2. Time Tracking: Monitoring how you spend your time throughout the day provides valuable data for assessing your time management skills. Use tools like time-tracking apps or simple spreadsheets to record activities and time spent on each task.

3. Feedback from Others: Colleagues, friends, or mentors can provide valuable insights into your time management skills from an external perspective. Seek feedback on your organizational skills, meeting deadlines, and task prioritization.

4. Objective Assessments: Several online assessments and quizzes are available to evaluate time management skills. These assessments often cover areas like task prioritization, goal setting, planning, and overcoming procrastination.

5. Metrics and Key Performance Indicators (KPIs): Establish metrics to measure your time management effectiveness, such as meeting deadlines, completing tasks within estimated time frames, or reducing time spent on non-essential activities.

Key Components of Time Management

1. Goal Setting: Effective time management begins with setting clear, measurable goals. Define short-term and long-term objectives to guide your daily activities and prioritize tasks accordingly.

2. Task Prioritization: Identify high-priority tasks that align with your goals and allocate time and resources accordingly. Use techniques like the Eisenhower Matrix to categorize tasks based on importance and urgency.

3. Planning and Scheduling: Develop a structured plan for your day, week, or month to allocate time for specific tasks. Use tools like calendars, to-do lists, and project management software to organize tasks and deadlines.

4. Time Blocking: Allocate dedicated time blocks for different activities, such as focused work, meetings, breaks, and personal tasks. This technique helps in maintaining focus and avoiding distractions.

5. Delegation and Outsourcing: Learn to delegate tasks that can be handled by others to free up your time for high-priority activities. Outsourcing non-essential tasks can also help in optimizing time management.

6. Effective Communication: Clear communication with team members, stakeholders, and peers is essential for managing expectations, avoiding misunderstandings, and ensuring smooth workflow.

Examples of Assessing Time Management Skills

1. Self-Assessment:
   - Example: You realize that you often underestimate the time needed to complete tasks, leading to last-minute rushes and incomplete work.
   - Action: Start tracking the time taken for each task to accurately estimate future deadlines and improve time management.

2. Feedback from Others:
   - Example: A colleague mentions that you frequently miss deadlines, causing delays in team projects.
   - Action: Seek advice on improving deadline management and consider adjusting your task prioritization.

3. Objective Assessments:

- Example: You take an online time management assessment that highlights your tendency to multitask and lose focus on important tasks.
- Action: Work on enhancing your focus by practicing mindfulness techniques or using productivity tools to minimize distractions.

4. Time Tracking:
- Example: You realize that a significant portion of your day is spent on non-essential activities like excessive social media usage.
- Action: Set limits on social media usage, implement time blocks for focused work, and track improvements in time allocation.

5. Metrics and KPIs:
- Example: You establish a KPI to reduce the time spent on unproductive meetings and track the percentage of time saved over a month.
- Action: Implement strategies like setting agendas, limiting meeting durations, and evaluating the impact on overall productivity.

Assessing your time management skills is an ongoing process that requires continuous evaluation, reflection, and adaptation. By identifying areas for improvement and implementing effective time management strategies, you can enhance productivity, reduce stress, and achieve your personal and professional goals more efficiently.

Strategies for Improving Time Management Skills

Once you have assessed your current time management skills, the next step is to implement strategies for improvement. Consider the following techniques to enhance your efficiency and productivity:

1. Set Clear Goals: Define specific, measurable goals to guide your daily activities. Break down larger goals into smaller tasks and prioritize them based on importance and urgency.

2. Establish Priorities: Identify high-priority tasks that align with your goals and focus on completing them first. Use techniques like the ABCDE method or the 80/20 rule to prioritize tasks effectively.

3. Create a Daily Schedule: Plan your day in advance by allocating time blocks for different activities. Use tools like calendars or time management apps to organize tasks and deadlines.

4. Avoid Multitasking: Focus on one task at a time to improve focus and productivity. Multitasking can lead to decreased efficiency and lower quality of work. Instead, practice single-tasking to enhance performance.

5. Manage Distractions: Identify common distractions in your work environment and take steps to minimize them. This can include turning off notifications, setting boundaries with colleagues, or creating a dedicated workspace.

6. Delegate Tasks: Learn to delegate tasks that can be handled

by others to free up your time for more important activities. Effective delegation helps in optimizing workload and improving overall productivity.

7. Use Time Management Tools: Utilize tools and apps designed to improve time management, such as task managers, calendars, and project management software. These tools can help in organizing tasks, setting reminders, and tracking progress.

8. Practice Time Blocking: Allocate specific time blocks for different activities, including focused work, meetings, breaks, and personal tasks. Time blocking helps in maintaining focus, reducing procrastination, and enhancing productivity.

9. Set Realistic Deadlines: Avoid overcommitting by setting realistic deadlines for tasks and projects. Consider factors like task complexity, resource availability, and your own capacity when establishing timelines.

10. Review and Reflect: Regularly review your progress and reflect on your time management habits. Identify what is working well and areas for improvement. Adjust your strategies based on feedback and results.

Example of Implementation

1. Setting Clear Goals:
   - Assessment: You realize that your goals are often vague or too broad, making it challenging to plan and prioritize tasks effectively.
   - Strategy: Break down your long-term goals into smaller,

actionable steps with specific deadlines. For example, instead of setting a goal to "improve sales," define specific targets such as "increase sales by 10% in the next quarter."

2. Creating a Daily Schedule:
  - Assessment: You find yourself frequently overwhelmed by the volume of tasks and deadlines, leading to last-minute rushes.
  - Strategy: Allocate time at the beginning or end of each day to plan and prioritize tasks for the next day. Use a planner or digital calendar to schedule specific time blocks for each task.

3. Managing Distractions:
  - Assessment: You notice that you often get sidetracked by incoming emails and notifications, disrupting your focus on important tasks.
  - Strategy: Implement strategies to reduce distractions, such as silencing notifications, setting specific email-checking times, and designating specific focus periods for deep work.

4. Practicing Time Blocking:
  - Assessment: You struggle with maintaining focus on tasks and tend to switch between activities frequently, affecting productivity.
  - Strategy: Implement a time-blocking technique where you allocate dedicated time blocks for different types of tasks throughout the day. Use this structured approach to focus on one task at a time without interruptions.

5. Regular Review and Reflection:
  - Assessment: You have been working on improving your

time management skills but are unsure about the effectiveness of your strategies.

- Strategy: Allocate time on a weekly or monthly basis to review your progress, evaluate the outcomes of your time management efforts, and identify areas for adjustment. Reflect on what worked well and what needs refinement to continuously improve.

Conclusion

Assessing your current time management skills is a critical step towards optimizing productivity, reducing stress, and achieving your goals more effectively. By reflecting on your time management habits, seeking feedback, and utilizing various assessment methods, you can gain valuable insights into areas for improvement.

Implementing strategies like setting clear goals, prioritizing tasks, creating schedules, managing distractions, and practicing time blocking can help you enhance your time management skills and boost your efficiency. Regular review and reflection on your progress allow you to adapt your strategies and continuously improve your time management practices.

Remember that effective time management is not a one-size-fits-all approach. It requires a personalized strategy tailored to your goals, preferences, and working style. By investing time and effort in assessing and improving your time management skills, you can unlock your full potential, accomplish more with less stress, and lead a more balanced and fulfilling life.

3

Setting Goals and Priorities

Setting goals and priorities is a fundamental aspect of personal and professional development that helps individuals achieve success in their endeavors. By defining clear objectives and determining what tasks are most important, individuals can focus their time, energy, and resources on activities that align with their values and objectives. In this comprehensive guide, we will explore the importance of setting goals and priorities, discuss strategies for effectively establishing them, and provide examples to illustrate how goal setting can lead to improved productivity and success.

Importance of Setting Goals and Priorities

Setting goals and priorities provides several benefits that contribute to personal growth and success. Some of the key reasons why establishing clear objectives is essential include:

1. Clarity and Focus: When individuals set specific goals, they gain clarity on what they want to achieve and the steps needed to

reach their objectives. This clarity helps them focus their efforts on tasks that are aligned with their goals, reducing distractions and increasing productivity.

2. Motivation: Goals provide motivation by giving individuals something to strive for and a sense of purpose. When individuals have clear goals in mind, they are more likely to stay motivated and committed to their pursuits, even when faced with challenges or setbacks.

3. Measuring Progress: By setting measurable goals, individuals can track their progress and assess how far they have come toward achieving their objectives. Regularly monitoring progress allows individuals to make adjustments as needed and stay on track to reach their goals.

4. Time Management: Establishing priorities helps individuals make informed decisions about how to allocate their time and resources. By identifying what tasks are most important, individuals can focus on high-impact activities that contribute to their overall success.

5. Accountability: Setting goals creates accountability by establishing clear expectations and deadlines for completing tasks. When individuals have goals in place, they are more likely to hold themselves accountable for their actions and strive to meet their objectives.

6. Personal Growth: Goal setting fosters personal growth and development by providing opportunities for individuals to challenge themselves and expand their skills and abilities.

Working toward challenging goals can help individuals build resilience, improve their problem-solving skills, and enhance their self-confidence.

Strategies for Setting Goals and Priorities

To effectively set goals and priorities, individuals can follow a systematic approach that includes the following strategies:

1. Define Your Objectives: Start by clarifying what you want to achieve and why it is important to you. Setting specific, measurable, achievable, relevant, and time-bound (SMART) goals can help you create clear objectives that guide your actions.

2. Prioritize Your Goals: Identify your most important goals and prioritize them based on their significance and impact on your life. Consider what goals align with your values, long-term vision, and current circumstances to determine which goals to focus on first.

3. Break Down Your Goals: Break down larger goals into smaller, manageable tasks that you can work on incrementally. This approach helps you avoid feeling overwhelmed and allows you to make progress step by step.

4. Set Deadlines: Establish deadlines for each goal or task to create a sense of urgency and accountability. Setting deadlines helps you stay on track and ensures that you make steady progress toward your objectives.

5. Create an Action Plan: Develop a detailed action plan out-

lining the specific steps you need to take to achieve each goal. Include milestones, deadlines, resources needed, and potential obstacles you may encounter along the way.

6. Monitor and Adjust: Regularly review your progress toward your goals and make adjustments as needed. If you encounter challenges or changes in your circumstances, be flexible and recalibrate your goals and priorities accordingly.

7. Celebrate Achievements: Acknowledge and celebrate your achievements as you reach milestones and complete goals. Recognizing your progress and successes can boost your motivation and inspire you to continue working toward your objectives.

Examples of Setting Goals and Priorities

To illustrate the concept of setting goals and priorities in action, let's consider a few examples across different contexts:

1. Personal Development:
   - Example: Sarah wants to improve her physical fitness and set a goal to run a half marathon in six months. She prioritizes her goal by creating a training schedule, joining a running group for support, and tracking her progress using a fitness app. By setting this goal, Sarah not only improves her physical health but also gains a sense of accomplishment and self-discipline.

2. Career Advancement:
   - Example: John aspires to advance in his career and become a manager within the next two years. He prioritizes his goal by enrolling in leadership development courses, seeking

mentorship from senior managers, and taking on additional responsibilities at work. By setting this goal, John demonstrates his commitment to professional growth and positions himself for future opportunities.

3. Academic Success:
   - Example: Emily aims to graduate with honors from college and secure a competitive internship in her field. She prioritizes her goal by creating a study schedule, seeking academic support when needed, and networking with professionals in her industry. By setting this goal, Emily maximizes her academic potential and enhances her future career prospects.

4. Financial Independence:
   - Example: Mark wants to achieve financial independence by saving a specific amount of money each month and investing in long-term assets. He prioritizes his goal by creating a budget, cutting unnecessary expenses, and seeking advice from financial advisors. By setting this goal, Mark takes proactive steps toward building wealth and securing his financial future.

Conclusion

In conclusion, setting goals and priorities is a strategic process that empowers individuals to achieve their aspirations and lead more fulfilling lives. By defining clear objectives, establishing priorities, and developing action plans, individuals can align their efforts with their values and objectives, leading to improved focus, productivity, and success. By following systematic strategies for goal setting and incorporating examples of setting goals and priorities in various contexts, individuals can leverage the power of goal setting to enhance their personal and professional growth. Embracing goal setting as a guiding principle can pave the way for continuous improvement, self-discovery, and ultimately, the realization of one's full potential.

4

Creating a Time Management Plan

Time management is a crucial skill that can significantly impact our productivity, efficiency, and overall well-being. Creating a time management plan is a strategic approach to organizing and prioritizing tasks to make the most of the limited time available. A well-structured time management plan helps individuals allocate their time effectively, reduce stress, improve focus, and achieve their goals more efficiently. In this detailed discussion, we will delve deep into the concept of time management plans, explore various strategies and techniques to create an effective plan, and provide practical examples to illustrate how to implement and optimize a time management plan in different contexts.

Understanding Time Management

Time management is the process of planning and organizing how to divide your time between specific activities. It involves setting goals, prioritizing tasks, and allocating resources like time and energy to accomplish those goals. Effective time management allows individuals to work smarter, not harder, ensuring that essential tasks are completed efficiently while avoiding wasting time on less critical activities.

Proper time management is essential in both personal and professional life. In personal life, managing time effectively can lead to a better work-life balance, reduced stress, and increased opportunities to pursue hobbies and interests. In a professional context, effective time management can boost productivity, enhance job satisfaction, and contribute to career advancement.

Benefits of Creating a Time Management Plan

1. Increased Productivity: A well-thought-out time management plan helps individuals focus on high-priority tasks and allocate time effectively, leading to increased productivity and efficiency in completing tasks.

2. Reduced Stress: By organizing tasks and setting clear deadlines, a time management plan can reduce stress levels associated with feeling overwhelmed or having to juggle multiple responsibilities.

3. Improved Focus: Setting specific goals and timelines enables individuals to concentrate on the task at hand without getting distracted by unrelated activities, thus improving focus and concentration.

4. Better Decision-Making: When time is managed effectively, individuals can make informed decisions about how to allocate their time and resources based on the importance and urgency

of tasks.

5. Achieving Goals: A time management plan helps individuals prioritize tasks aligned with their goals, making it easier to make progress towards achieving those goals.

Components of a Time Management Plan

Creating a time management plan involves several key components that help individuals structure their tasks and allocate time efficiently. Some essential components of a time management plan include:

1. Task Identification: Listing all tasks and activities that need to be completed, including both short-term and long-term commitments.

2. Priority Setting: Prioritizing tasks based on their importance and deadlines, categorizing them as high, medium, or low priority.

3. Time Allocation: Allocating specific time blocks for each task or activity, ensuring that enough time is allotted to complete high-priority tasks.

4. Goal Setting: Setting specific, achievable goals to guide task prioritization and overall time management efforts.

5. Scheduling: Creating a daily, weekly, or monthly schedule to plan and organize tasks, meetings, and other commitments effectively.

6. Tracking Progress: Monitoring and tracking progress on tasks to ensure that deadlines are met and goals are achieved.

7. Flexibility: Building in flexibility to accommodate unexpected events or changes in priorities that may arise during the day.

Strategies for Creating an Effective Time Management Plan

To create an effective time management plan, individuals can adopt various strategies and techniques that help streamline their workflow, prioritize tasks, and optimize their time usage. Here are some strategies for creating an efficient time management plan:

1. Set Clear Goals: Start by defining specific, measurable goals that you want to achieve within a given timeframe. Clearly defined goals provide a sense of direction and purpose, making it easier to prioritize tasks effectively.

2. Identify Important Tasks: Make a list of all tasks and activities that need to be completed, categorizing them based on their importance and urgency. This will help you focus on high-priority tasks and avoid wasting time on less critical activities.

3. Utilize Time Management Tools: Take advantage of digital tools and apps designed for time management, such as task managers, calendars, and productivity apps. These tools can help you organize tasks, set reminders, and track progress efficiently.

4. Prioritize Tasks: Prioritize tasks based on their importance

and deadlines, focusing on completing high-priority tasks first before moving on to less critical activities. The Eisenhower Matrix, which categorizes tasks into four quadrants based on importance and urgency, can be a useful tool for prioritization.

5. Allocate Time Wisely: Allocate specific time blocks for each task or activity, ensuring that you dedicate enough time to complete high-priority tasks. Use techniques like time blocking or the Pomodoro Technique to manage your time effectively and maintain focus.

6. Avoid Multitasking: While multitasking may seem productive, it can actually reduce efficiency and quality of work. Focus on one task at a time to maintain concentration and complete tasks more effectively.

7. Minimize Distractions: Identify and minimize distractions in your workspace that can disrupt your focus and productivity. Consider using techniques like time blocking, setting boundaries, or implementing digital detox periods to reduce distractions.

8. Regular Breaks: Schedule regular breaks between tasks to recharge and maintain energy levels throughout the day. Short breaks can help improve focus, productivity, and overall well-being.

9. Review and Adjust: Regularly review your time management plan and make adjustments as needed based on changes in priorities, deadlines, or unexpected events. Continuous improvement is key to optimizing your time management

approach.

10. Practice Time Management Skills: Developing time management skills requires practice and consistency. Start implementing your time management plan gradually, focusing on small changes that can lead to long-term improvements in productivity and efficiency.

Examples of Implementing a Time Management Plan

To better understand how to create and implement a time management plan, let's consider some practical examples illustrating the application of time management strategies in different contexts:

Example 1: College Student Time Management Plan

Scenario: Sarah is a college student with multiple assignments, exams, and extracurricular activities to balance. She wants to create a time management plan to effectively manage her academic and personal responsibilities.

1. Goal Setting: Sarah sets specific goals for each week, including completing assignments before the deadline, studying for exams in advance, and participating in at least two extracurricular activities.

2. Task Identification: She identifies all upcoming assignments and exams, categorizing them based on their deadlines and importance.

3. Priority Setting: Sarah prioritizes tasks based on their deadlines and importance, focusing on completing assignments first before studying for exams.

4. Time Allocation: She allocates specific time blocks for each task, such as dedicating two hours each day to studying and completing assignments.

5. Scheduling: Sarah creates a weekly schedule that includes study sessions, assignment deadlines, and extracurricular activities, ensuring she has enough time for each task.

6. Tracking Progress: She monitors her progress on assignments and exams, adjusting her schedule as needed to meet deadlines and achieve her goals.

By following this time management plan, Sarah can effectively balance her academic workload and personal activities while staying focused and motivated to achieve her goals.

Example 2: Remote Worker Time Management Plan

Scenario: John works remotely as a freelance graphic designer, juggling multiple client projects and deadlines. He struggles with maintaining focus and managing his time effectively while working from home.

1. Set Clear Goals: John defines specific project goals and deadlines for each client, ensuring he has a clear direction for his work.

2. Identify Important Tasks: He lists all client projects, categorizing them based on their urgency and complexity to prioritize tasks effectively.

3. Utilize Time Management Tools: John uses project management tools like Trello and time tracking apps to organize tasks, set reminders, and track his progress on client projects.

4. Prioritize Tasks: He prioritizes tasks based on client deadlines and project requirements, focusing on completing high-priority projects first.

5. Allocate Time Wisely: John allocates specific time blocks for each project, using time blocking to dedicate uninterrupted time to focus on individual client tasks.

6. Minimize Distractions: He creates a dedicated workspace free from distractions, sets boundaries with family members, and implements regular breaks to maintain focus and productivity.

7. Review and Adjust: John regularly reviews his project timelines and adjusts his schedule as needed based on client feedback, changes in priorities, or unexpected events.

By implementing this time management plan, John can streamline his workflow, meet client deadlines efficiently, and maintain a healthy work-life balance while working remotely.

Challenges of Implementing a Time Management Plan

While creating a time management plan can offer numerous

benefits, individuals may encounter various challenges when implementing and sustaining their time management efforts. Some common challenges associated with time management plans include:

1. Procrastination: Procrastination can hinder productivity and time management efforts, leading to delays in completing tasks and achieving goals.

2. Overcommitting: Taking on too many tasks or commitments can result in overwhelm and difficulty managing time effectively, impacting overall productivity.

3. Interruptions and Distractions: Unexpected interruptions and distractions can disrupt focus and workflow, affecting the ability to manage time efficiently.

4. Lack of Flexibility: A rigid time management plan may not account for unexpected events or changes in priorities, making it challenging to adapt to unforeseen circumstances.

5. Poor Planning: Ineffective planning and time allocation can lead to inefficiencies, missed deadlines, and difficulty in achieving goals.

To overcome these challenges, individuals can implement strategies like setting realistic goals, practicing self-discipline, minimizing distractions, and building in flexibility to adapt to changing circumstances.

Conclusion

In conclusion, creating a time management plan is a vital step towards optimizing productivity, reducing stress, and achieving goals effectively. By understanding the core principles of time management, adopting strategic planning techniques, and implementing practical strategies, individuals can structure their tasks, prioritize activities, and manage their time efficiently to accomplish more in less time.

An effective time management plan involves setting clear goals, identifying important tasks, allocating time wisely, and utilizing time management tools to streamline workflow and enhance productivity. By applying time management strategies in various contexts, such as academic settings, remote work environments, or personal life, individuals can tailor their approach to suit their unique needs and goals.

While challenges may arise when implementing a time management plan, individuals can overcome obstacles by practicing self-discipline, minimizing distractions, and maintaining flexibility to adapt to changing circumstances. Continuous improvement and consistent practice of time management skills are key to long-term success in managing time effectively and achieving desired outcomes.

By creating and implementing a personalized time management plan tailored to individual needs and preferences, individuals can unlock their full potential, maximize productivity, and lead a more balanced and fulfilling life.

5

Overcoming Procrastination

Procrastination is a common behavior that many people struggle with at various points in their lives. It involves delaying or postponing tasks or activities that need to be accomplished, often opting for more pleasurable or less demanding activities instead. Overcoming procrastination is a challenge that requires self-awareness, motivation, and effective strategies to change one's habits and improve productivity.

In this deep dive, we will explore various aspects of procrastination, including its causes, consequences, and ways to overcome it. By understanding the root causes of procrastination and learning practical techniques to combat it, individuals can increase their efficiency, reduce stress, and achieve their goals more effectively.

Understanding Procrastination

Procrastination is a complex phenomenon influenced by a combination of internal and external factors. Some common reasons people procrastinate include:

1. Fear of Failure: One of the most significant underlying causes of procrastination is the fear of not meeting expectations or failing at a task. This fear can lead individuals to put off starting or completing a task to avoid potential disappointment or criticism.

Example: An employee may delay working on a challenging project because they fear making mistakes or not meeting their manager's expectations.

2. Perfectionism: Perfectionists often struggle with procrastination because they set unrealistically high standards for themselves. The fear of not being able to meet these standards can lead to avoidance and delay in starting tasks.

Example: A student may procrastinate on writing a research paper because they feel overwhelmed by the pressure to produce a flawless piece of work.

3. Lack of Motivation: When individuals lack interest or motivation in a task, they may procrastinate to avoid engaging with something they find boring or unfulfilling.

Example: A person may put off cleaning their house because they do not enjoy the task and do not see immediate benefits from doing it.

4. Task Difficulty: Tasks that are perceived as complex, unclear, or overwhelming can trigger procrastination. Individuals may delay starting such tasks due to the perceived effort required to complete them.

Example: A small business owner may procrastinate on developing a new marketing strategy because they find the process daunting and time-consuming.

5. Poor Time Management: Ineffective time management skills can also contribute to procrastination. Without a clear plan or schedule, individuals may struggle to prioritize tasks and allocate their time effectively.

Example: A freelancer may delay working on multiple projects because they have not established a structured schedule for completing each task.

Consequences of Procrastination
Procrastination can have a range of negative consequences that impact various aspects of an individual's life. Some common consequences of procrastination include:

1. Increased Stress and Anxiety: Procrastination often leads to increased stress as deadlines approach and tasks remain unfinished. The anxiety caused by pending tasks can have long-lasting effects on an individual's mental well-being.

2. Reduced Productivity: Procrastination hinders productivity by delaying the completion of essential tasks. This can lead to missed opportunities, decreased efficiency, and a sense of underachievement.

3. Poor Quality of Work: Rushing to complete tasks at the last minute due to procrastination can result in a lower quality of work. Lack of sufficient time for planning and reflection may

compromise the final outcome.

4. Damaged Relationships: Procrastination can strain relationships with colleagues, friends, or family members. Missing deadlines or failing to follow through on commitments can erode trust and lead to conflicts.

5. Missed Opportunities: Procrastination can result in missed opportunities for personal and professional growth. Delaying actions that could lead to advancement or success may limit one's potential.

6. Physical Health Effects: Chronic procrastination has been linked to negative physical health outcomes, such as disrupted sleep patterns, increased fatigue, and other stress-related ailments.

Strategies for Overcoming Procrastination

While overcoming procrastination can be challenging, several strategies and techniques can help individuals break the cycle of delay and improve their productivity. Here are some effective approaches to conquer procrastination:

1. Set Clear Goals and Priorities: Establishing clear, specific goals and priorities can help individuals focus their efforts and avoid getting overwhelmed by the magnitude of tasks. Break down larger goals into smaller, manageable steps to make progress more achievable.

Example: Instead of setting a vague goal like "Finish project X," specify tasks like "Research topic for project X" or "Draft outline for project X" to create a roadmap for completion.

2. Create a Structured Schedule: Develop a daily or weekly schedule that allocates dedicated time blocks for tasks and activities. Prioritize important tasks and set realistic deadlines to ensure steady progress.

Example: Use a planner or digital calendar to map out your day, scheduling specific times for work, breaks, exercise, and leisure activities. Stick to the schedule as closely as possible to build consistency.

3. Utilize Time Management Techniques: Employ proven time management techniques, such as the Pomodoro Technique (working in focused intervals with short breaks) or the Eisenhower Matrix (prioritizing tasks based on urgency and importance), to enhance productivity and avoid procrastination.

Example: Divide your work into 25-minute intervals of focused work (Pomodoro sessions) followed by 5-minute breaks to maintain concentration and momentum throughout the day.

4. Practice Self-Compassion: Be kind to yourself and acknowledge that occasional procrastination is a common experience. Avoid self-criticism and negative self-talk, which can further impede progress. Instead, cultivate self-compassion and learn from setbacks to improve future performance.

Example: When you catch yourself procrastinating, practice self-compassion by saying, "It's okay to make mistakes. What can I learn from this experience to do better next time?"

5. Use Visualization and Affirmations: Visualizing yourself successfully completing tasks can boost motivation and reduce procrastination. Positive affirmations and visual cues can help reinforce your commitment to achieving your goals.

Example: Create a vision board with images or words representing your goals and aspirations. Use affirmations like "I am capable of overcoming obstacles" to stay focused and motivated.

6. Break Tasks into Smaller Steps: When faced with a daunting or overwhelming task, break it down into smaller, actionable steps. By focusing on completing one step at a time, you can build momentum and make progress more manageable.

Example: Instead of trying to tackle an entire project at once, break it down into research, outline, drafting, editing, and final review stages to simplify the process.

7. Eliminate Distractions: Identify and eliminate distractions in your environment that contribute to procrastination. Turn off notifications, create a quiet workspace, and establish boundaries to minimize interruptions and stay focused on your tasks.

Example: Put your phone on silent, close unnecessary tabs on your computer, and inform colleagues or family members about your focused work periods to reduce distractions and enhance concentration.

8. Reward Progress: Celebrate small victories and milestones along the way to keep yourself motivated and engaged with your tasks. Rewarding progress can reinforce positive behavior

and make the process of overcoming procrastination more enjoyable.

Example: Treat yourself to a favorite snack, take a short break to relax, or engage in a fun activity after completing a challenging task to recognize your efforts and maintain momentum.

9. Seek Accountability: Share your goals and deadlines with a friend, mentor, or colleague who can provide support and hold you accountable for your progress. Regular check-ins and feedback can help you stay motivated and committed to your goals.

Example: Form a study group with classmates to keep each other accountable for completing assignments and preparing for exams. Share progress updates and offer support to one another to stay on track.

10. Practice Mindfulness and Stress Management: Incorporate mindfulness practices, such as deep breathing exercises, meditation, or yoga, to reduce stress and increase focus. Mindfulness can help you stay present, manage overwhelming emotions, and improve decision-making.

Example: Take brief mindfulness breaks throughout the day to center yourself and refocus your attention. Practice deep breathing exercises or guided meditation to quiet your mind and alleviate stress before tackling challenging tasks.

Conclusion

Overcoming procrastination requires a combination of self-awareness, motivation, and effective strategies to change ingrained habits and improve productivity. By understanding the root causes of procrastination, recognizing its consequences, and implementing practical techniques to combat it, individuals can enhance their time management skills, reduce stress, and achieve their goals more efficiently.

Whether it involves setting clear goals, creating structured schedules, practicing self-compassion, or seeking external accountability, the journey to overcoming procrastination is a personal and ongoing process. By applying the strategies outlined in this deep dive and adapting them to suit your unique circumstances, you can develop a proactive approach to task management and experience the satisfaction of increased productivity and accomplishment.

Remember that overcoming procrastination is not about achieving perfection or eliminating all delays but rather about cultivating resilience, consistency, and a positive mindset to navigate challenges and setbacks effectively. With perseverance and a willingness to learn from each experience, you can gradually diminish the impact of procrastination on your life and work towards realizing your full potential.

6

Delegating and Outsourcing Tasks

Delegating and outsourcing tasks are essential strategies used by individuals and organizations to improve efficiency, productivity, and focus on core activities. Delegating involves assigning tasks to others within the same organization, while outsourcing involves contracting a third-party external provider to complete tasks or provide services. Both strategies have their benefits and challenges, and understanding when and how to delegate or outsource can significantly impact an individual or organization's success.

Delegating Tasks:

Delegating tasks within an organization involves assigning specific responsibilities or projects to employees or team members. Effective delegation allows leaders to distribute workload, capitalize on team members' strengths, and create opportunities for professional growth and skill development. Here are some key points to consider when delegating tasks:

1. Clear Communication: When delegating tasks, it is crucial to communicate clearly the expectations, goals, deadlines, and any other relevant information to the team members. Ambiguity in instructions can lead to misunderstandings and errors.

2. Assigning Appropriately: Understanding team members' skills, strengths, and availability is crucial in delegating tasks effectively. Assigning tasks that align with individuals' capabilities can improve efficiency and ensure successful completion.

3. Providing Support: While delegating tasks, it is important to provide necessary support, resources, and guidance to team members. Regular check-ins, feedback, and assistance can help team members overcome challenges and achieve their goals.

4. Empowering Team Members: Delegating tasks is not just about assigning work but also empowering team members to make decisions, solve problems, and take ownership of their responsibilities. Empowered employees are more motivated and engaged in their work.

5. Accountability and Feedback: Establishing clear accountability for delegated tasks and providing regular feedback on performance are essential for successful delegation. Recognizing achievements and addressing issues promptly can improve team members' performance and confidence.

Examples of Delegating Tasks:

1. Project Management: A project manager delegates specific tasks to team members based on their expertise and availability.

For example, assigning research tasks to a team member with strong analytical skills and coordinating deadlines for various project milestones.

2. Employee Development: A manager delegates training tasks to team members to enhance their skills and knowledge in a particular area. For instance, assigning a team member to lead a presentation skills workshop for the department.

3. Administrative Tasks: A supervisor delegates administrative tasks such as scheduling meetings, organizing files, or responding to emails to an administrative assistant to streamline workflow and free up time for strategic activities.

4. Customer Service: A customer service manager delegates handling customer inquiries or complaints to team members based on their experience and communication skills to ensure timely and effective resolution.

Outsourcing Tasks:

Outsourcing involves contracting external vendors or service providers to complete specific tasks or services that are not within the organization's core competencies. Outsourcing allows organizations to access specialized expertise, reduce costs, improve efficiency, and focus on strategic priorities. Here are some key considerations when outsourcing tasks:

1. Define Scope and Objectives: Before outsourcing tasks, organizations should clearly define the scope, objectives, deliverables, and expectations to align with the vendor. A well-defined

outsourcing agreement helps prevent misunderstandings and ensures successful collaboration.

2. Vendor Selection: Choosing the right vendor with the necessary expertise, experience, and reliability is crucial in outsourcing tasks effectively. Conducting due diligence, reference checks, and evaluating vendors' capabilities can help organizations make informed decisions.

3. Contracts and Agreements: Formalizing outsourcing agreements through contracts that outline terms, conditions, responsibilities, timelines, and confidentiality agreements is essential. Clear contractual agreements protect both parties and establish a framework for collaboration.

4. Communication and Collaboration: Effective communication and collaboration with outsourced vendors are vital for successful task completion. Regular updates, feedback sessions, and status reports facilitate transparency and alignment between the organization and the vendor.

5. Quality Assurance: Monitoring and evaluating the quality of work delivered by outsourced vendors are critical to ensure compliance with standards, requirements, and expectations. Implementing quality assurance measures can help maintain consistency and reliability in outsourced tasks.

Examples of Outsourcing Tasks:

1. Information Technology: Organizations may outsource IT services such as software development, network management,

cybersecurity, or help desk support to specialized IT firms to leverage expertise and technology infrastructure.

2. Human Resources: Outsourcing HR functions like payroll processing, recruitment, training, or benefits administration to external HR firms can help organizations streamline HR processes and compliance requirements.

3. Marketing and Advertising: Businesses often outsource marketing and advertising activities such as social media management, content creation, graphic design, or digital campaigns to marketing agencies for branding and lead generation.

4. Accounting and Finance: Outsourcing accounting services like bookkeeping, financial reporting, tax preparation, or auditing to accounting firms can help organizations comply with financial regulations and improve financial management.

Benefits of Delegating and Outsourcing Tasks:

Both delegating and outsourcing tasks offer numerous benefits for individuals and organizations, including:

1. Improved Efficiency: Delegating tasks allows individuals to focus on high-priority activities, while outsourcing specific tasks to external vendors leverages specialized expertise, leading to increased efficiency in task completion.

2. Cost Savings: Outsourcing tasks can help organizations reduce operational costs, overhead expenses, and labor costs associated with hiring and training additional staff. Delegating

tasks within the organization optimizes resource allocation and productivity.

3. Access to Expertise: Outsourcing tasks to external vendors grants access to specialized skills, knowledge, technologies, and resources that may not be available internally. Delegating tasks based on team members' skills and strengths leverages internal expertise for improved performance.

4. Scalability and Flexibility: Delegating and outsourcing tasks offer scalability and flexibility for organizations to adapt to changing business needs, fluctuations in workload, or new project requirements without compromising quality or efficiency.

5. Focus on Core Activities: Delegating non-core tasks and outsourcing specialized functions allow organizations to concentrate on strategic priorities, innovation, growth initiatives, and core competencies for long-term success.

Challenges of Delegating and Outsourcing Tasks:

While delegating and outsourcing tasks offer various benefits, they also present challenges that need to be addressed for successful implementation, including:

1. Loss of Control: Delegating tasks within the organization or outsourcing to external vendors may result in a perceived loss of control over task execution, quality standards, timelines, or outcomes. Clear communication, monitoring, and collaboration help mitigate this risk.

2. Communication Issues: Inadequate communication, misalignment of expectations, cultural differences, or language barriers can lead to misunderstandings, delays, errors, or conflicts in task delegation and outsourcing. Effective communication strategies are essential for successful collaboration.

3. Quality Concerns: Ensuring the quality of work delivered by team members or outsourced vendors can be a challenge due to differences in standards, preferences, or capabilities. Implementing quality assurance measures and feedback mechanisms can address quality concerns.

4. Dependency on Vendors: Organizations relying heavily on outsourced vendors for critical functions or tasks may face risks related to vendor dependency, supplier stability, contract renegotiations, or transitioning to new vendors in case of disruptions.

5. Employee Morale: Delegating tasks within the organization without adequate support, training, recognition, or career development opportunities can impact employee morale, job satisfaction, and engagement. Acknowledging and rewarding team members for delegated responsibilities can help boost morale.

In conclusion, delegating and outsourcing tasks are valuable strategies that individuals and organizations can utilize to optimize productivity, efficiency, and focus on core activities. By effectively delegating tasks within the organization and outsourcing specific functions to external vendors, individuals and organizations can leverage internal expertise, access external resources, enhance scalability, and achieve strategic objectives. Understanding the benefits, challenges, best practices, and considerations associated with delegating and outsourcing tasks is essential for making informed decisions, optimizing workflow, and driving success in a dynamic and competitive business environment.

7

Time Management Tools and Techniques

Time management is a crucial skill in today's fast-paced world where we are constantly bombarded with various tasks, responsibilities, and distractions. Effectively managing our time can lead to increased productivity, reduced stress, and overall better work-life balance. To help individuals and teams manage their time more efficiently, a variety of tools and techniques have been developed. In this comprehensive guide, we will delve deeply into the various time management tools and techniques available, providing detailed explanations and examples to help you optimize your time effectively.

Part 1: Time Management Tools

1.1: To-Do Lists

One of the most common and effective time management tools is the humble to-do list. To-do lists help individuals organize their tasks, set priorities, and track their progress throughout the day. There are various approaches to creating to-do lists, including traditional pen-and-paper lists, digital to-do list apps, and task management tools like Trello and Asana.

Example:
Sarah starts her day by making a to-do list in her favorite task management app. She categorizes tasks by priority and deadlines, ensuring that she focuses on the most important tasks first.

1.2: Calendar Apps

Calendar apps are essential time management tools that help individuals schedule appointments, meetings, and tasks. They allow users to set reminders, allocate specific time slots for each activity, and visualize their daily, weekly, or monthly schedule.

Example:
John uses Google Calendar to plan his week in advance, setting aside dedicated time blocks for work-related tasks, exercise, and personal activities.

1.3: Pomodoro Technique

The Pomodoro Technique is a time management method that breaks work into intervals (typically 25 minutes) separated by short breaks. This technique aims to improve focus and productivity by allowing individuals to work in concentrated bursts.

Example:
Anna uses a Pomodoro timer app to work on her report in

25-minute intervals, followed by 5-minute breaks. She finds that this technique helps her maintain focus and complete tasks efficiently.

1.4: Time Tracking Software

Time tracking software enables individuals to monitor how they spend their time throughout the day. By tracking activities and analyzing time usage, users can identify areas of improvement and optimize their workflow.

Example:
   David uses a time tracking tool to log time spent on different projects and tasks. By reviewing his time data, he identifies time-wasting activities and adjusts his schedule accordingly.

1.5: Task Management Apps

Task management apps like Todoist, Microsoft To Do, and Wunderlist help individuals organize, prioritize, and track their tasks effectively. These apps often include features such as task due dates, reminders, subtasks, and collaboration tools.

Example:
   Emily utilizes a task management app to create project-specific task lists, assign priorities, and share tasks with her team members. This helps her team stay organized and meet project deadlines.

Part 2: Time Management Techniques

2.1: Eisenhower Matrix

The Eisenhower Matrix, also known as the Urgent-Important Matrix, is a time management technique that categorizes tasks into four quadrants based on their urgency and importance. This method helps individuals prioritize tasks and focus on what truly matters.

Example:
Michael uses the Eisenhower Matrix to differentiate between urgent tasks that require immediate attention and important tasks that contribute to his long-term goals. This technique helps him allocate his time wisely and avoid procrastination.

2.2: Eat That Frog

The "Eat That Frog" technique, popularized by Brian Tracy, encourages individuals to tackle their most challenging or important task first thing in the morning. By completing the most difficult task early in the day, individuals can build momentum and enhance their productivity.

Example:
Sophia follows the "Eat That Frog" technique by starting her day with the most daunting task on her to-do list. She finds that by tackling the task head-on, she feels a sense of accomplishment and motivation to tackle other tasks efficiently.

2.3: Time Blocking

Time blocking is a time management technique that involves

scheduling specific time blocks for different tasks or activities. By setting aside dedicated time periods for focused work, meetings, and breaks, individuals can enhance their productivity and organization.

Example:

Mark practices time blocking by allocating morning hours for focused work on important projects, mid-day slots for meetings, and afternoon blocks for personal tasks and leisure activities. This technique helps him maintain a structured daily routine.

2.4: Single-Tasking

Single-tasking is the practice of focusing on one task at a time without distractions. This time management technique promotes deep work, reduces multitasking-induced stress, and improves overall attention and productivity.

Example:

Jessica adopts the single-tasking approach by turning off notifications, silencing her phone, and dedicating uninterrupted time to complete a task. By concentrating on one task at a time, she achieves higher quality results in less time.

2.5: Getting Things Done (GTD)

The Getting Things Done (GTD) method, developed by David Allen, is a comprehensive time management system that emphasizes capturing, organizing, and prioritizing tasks. GTD encourages individuals to clear their minds of clutter and focus on actionable steps to achieve their goals.

Example:

Alex implements the GTD method by regularly collecting and categorizing his tasks, setting specific next actions, and reviewing his task lists. This systematic approach helps him stay on top of his commitments and reduce mental overwhelm.

Part 3: Integrating Tools and Techniques

To maximize the benefits of time management, individuals can combine different tools and techniques based on their preferences and work styles. For example, utilizing a combination of to-do lists, calendar apps, and the Pomodoro Technique can help individuals plan their day, allocate time effectively, and maintain focus on tasks. By experimenting with various tools and techniques, individuals can identify what works best for them and establish a customized time management system that aligns with their goals and priorities.

Conclusion

In conclusion, effective time management is essential for improving productivity, reducing stress, and achieving work-life balance. By leveraging a diverse range of time management tools and techniques such as to-do lists, calendar apps, the Pomodoro Technique, the Eisenhower Matrix, and time blocking, individuals can optimize their time, prioritize tasks, and enhance their overall efficiency. By integrating these tools and techniques into their daily routines, individuals can cultivate better time management habits and effectively manage their workload and commitments. Remember that time management is a skill that can be developed and refined over time, so experiment with different tools and techniques to find what works best for you.

8

Managing Distractions and Interruptions

Managing distractions and interruptions is a crucial skill in today's fast-paced world where we are constantly bombarded with information and stimuli. Whether you are a student trying to focus on studying, an employee working on a project, or just trying to be present in the moment, distractions and interruptions can derail your productivity and focus. In this comprehensive guide, we will delve deeply into the topic of managing distractions and interruptions, exploring various strategies, techniques, and tools that can help you stay focused and productive.

Understanding Distractions and Interruptions

Before we discuss how to manage distractions and interruptions, it is important to understand what they are and how they impact our cognitive processes and productivity.

Distractions can come in many forms, such as noises, notifications, environmental stimuli, or internal thoughts. They divert our attention away from the task at hand and can make it difficult to maintain focus. Distractions can be both external and internal. External distractions are physical interruptions in our environment, like a loud conversation in the background, while internal distractions are thoughts or emotions that intrude on our mental space, such as worrying about a deadline or thinking about what to cook for dinner.

Interruptions, on the other hand, are more sudden and pronounced breaks in our focus caused by an external event or interaction. Interruptions can come in the form of phone calls, emails, colleagues stopping by your desk, or any other unexpected event that requires your immediate attention. While some interruptions are unavoidable and may require an immediate response, others can be managed or minimized with the right strategies.

The Impact of Distractions and Interruptions

Distractions and interruptions can have a significant impact on our cognitive performance and overall well-being. Here are some ways in which they can affect us:

1. Reduced Productivity: When we are constantly distracted or interrupted, it can take us longer to complete tasks and achieve our goals. Our brains need time to refocus and get back on track after an interruption, which can lead to a loss of productive time.

2. Increased Stress: Dealing with frequent distractions and interruptions can be stressful and overwhelming. It can make us feel like we are constantly playing catch-up and never fully

in control of our time and attention.

3. Decreased Focus and Concentration: Distractions can make it difficult to concentrate on the task at hand, leading to reduced quality of work and increased errors. Interruptions can break our train of thought and make it challenging to regain our focus.

4. Negative Impact on Health: Chronic exposure to distractions and interruptions can have a negative impact on our physical and mental health. It can lead to increased stress levels, fatigue, anxiety, and even burnout in the long run.

Strategies for Managing Distractions and Interruptions

Now that we have a better understanding of distractions and interruptions and their potential impact, let's explore some effective strategies for managing them:

1. Create a Distraction-Free Environment: One of the most effective ways to tackle distractions is to create a physical environment that is conducive to focus. This may involve finding a quiet space to work, using noise-canceling headphones, or decluttering your workspace to minimize visual distractions.

2. Set Clear Goals and Priorities: Having clear goals and priorities can help you stay on track and avoid getting sidetracked by distractions. Break down your tasks into smaller, manageable steps and prioritize them based on importance and urgency.

3. Time Blocking: Time blocking is a technique where you schedule specific blocks of time for different tasks or activi-

ties. By setting aside dedicated time for focused work without interruptions, you can increase your productivity and efficiency.

4. Use Time Management Techniques: Time management techniques, such as the Pomodoro Technique or the Eisenhower Matrix, can help you prioritize tasks, manage your time effectively, and stay focused on what matters most.

5. Limit Multitasking: Multitasking can actually decrease productivity and increase the likelihood of distractions and interruptions. Focus on one task at a time and give it your full attention before moving on to the next task.

6. Practice Mindfulness: Mindfulness techniques, such as deep breathing, meditation, or body scans, can help you stay present in the moment and reduce the impact of distractions on your focus and concentration.

7. Use Technology Mindfully: While technology can be a source of distractions, it can also be a helpful tool for managing interruptions. Use features like "Do Not Disturb" mode, app blockers, or productivity apps to limit distractions and stay focused on your work.

8. Establish Boundaries: Set boundaries with colleagues, friends, and family members to minimize interruptions during your focused work time. Communicate your availability and preferred modes of communication to reduce unnecessary interruptions.

9. Take Breaks: Regular breaks are essential for maintaining focus and productivity. Schedule short breaks between work

sessions to rest and recharge, allowing your brain to recover from intense focus.

10. Practice Self-Care: Prioritize self-care activities, such as exercise, healthy eating, and adequate sleep, to improve your overall well-being and resilience to distractions and interruptions.

Case Studies: Examples of Managing Distractions and Interruptions

Let's explore some real-life case studies and examples of individuals and organizations effectively managing distractions and interruptions:

Case Study 1: Remote Worker Managing Digital Distractions

Background: Sarah is a remote worker who struggles with digital distractions while working from home. She finds it challenging to stay focused on her tasks with constant email notifications, social media alerts, and messages from colleagues.

Solution: Sarah decides to implement the following strategies to manage digital distractions effectively:

- Turn Off Notifications: Sarah turns off non-essential notifications on her phone and computer to limit interruptions during focused work time.
- Use Website Blockers: Sarah installs a website blocker extension on her browser to block distracting websites during work hours.

- Implement the Pomodoro Technique: Sarah uses the Pomodoro Technique to work in focused 25-minute intervals with short breaks in between.

Outcome: By implementing these strategies, Sarah notices a significant improvement in her focus and productivity. She is able to complete her tasks more efficiently and with fewer interruptions, leading to a sense of accomplishment and reduced stress.

Case Study 2: Team Collaboration in an Open Office Setting

Background: A marketing team works in an open office setting where interruptions are common due to frequent interactions among team members. The team members find it challenging to balance collaborative work with individual tasks.

Solution: The team decides to implement the following strategies to manage interruptions and maintain focus:

- Designated Quiet Zones: The team designates specific areas in the office as quiet zones where team members can work without interruptions.
- Scheduled Collaboration Time: The team schedules dedicated time for collaborative work and meetings to minimize interruptions during individual focused work time.
- Use of Collaboration Tools: The team utilizes digital collaboration tools, such as project management software and communication platforms, to streamline communication and reduce interruptions.

Outcome: By creating a balance between collaborative work and individual focused work, the team is able to improve productivity and efficiency. Team members feel more in control of their time and are better able to manage interruptions while maintaining a collaborative work environment.

Case Study 3: Student Managing Study Distractions

Background: Alex is a student preparing for final exams and struggles to stay focused while studying at home. He finds himself easily distracted by his phone, social media, and household chores.

Solution: Alex implements the following strategies to manage study distractions effectively:

- Create a Study Schedule: Alex creates a study schedule with dedicated blocks of time for each subject and topic, eliminating the need for decision-making during study sessions.
- Use the 5-Minute Rule: Alex commits to studying for at least 5 minutes without distractions before taking a break or attending to other tasks.
- Physical Environment Optimization: Alex sets up a study area free from clutter and distractions, with minimal access to his phone and other potential distractors.

Outcome: By implementing these strategies, Alex experiences improved focus and concentration while studying. He is able to retain information better and make efficient progress in his exam preparation.

Tools and Techniques for Managing Distractions and Interruptions

In addition to the strategies and case studies mentioned above, there are several tools and techniques that can help you manage distractions and interruptions effectively. Here are some popular tools and techniques:

1. Pomodoro Technique: The Pomodoro Technique is a time management method that involves working in focused intervals (usually 25 minutes) followed by short breaks. It can help you stay productive and maintain focus on your tasks.

2. Website Blockers: Website blocker tools, such as StayFocusd, Freedom, or Cold Turkey, allow you to block access to distracting websites or apps during designated work hours.

3. Productivity Apps: Productivity apps like Todoist, Trello, or Asana can help you organize your tasks, set priorities, and stay focused on your goals.

4. Noise-Canceling Headphones: Noise-canceling headphones can help block out background noise and create a distraction-free environment for focused work.

5. Digital Detox Tools: Digital detox tools, such as Forest or Flipd, encourage you to stay off your devices and avoid digital distractions during work or study sessions.

6. Mindfulness Apps: Mindfulness apps like Headspace or Calm can help you practice meditation, deep breathing, and other

mindfulness techniques to reduce stress and improve focus.

7. Email Management Tools: Email management tools like Boomerang or Unroll.Me can help you organize your inbox, schedule emails, and reduce the frequency of interruptions from incoming messages.

Conclusion

Managing distractions and interruptions is an essential skill in today's busy world, where our attention is constantly pulled in multiple directions. By understanding the impact of distractions and interruptions on our productivity and well-being and implementing effective strategies, techniques, and tools, we can improve our focus, concentration, and overall performance. Whether you are a student, an employee, or an individual seeking to enhance your productivity, the ability to manage distractions and interruptions is a valuable asset that can help you achieve your goals and thrive in today's fast-paced environment.

9

Maintaining Work-Life Balance

Maintaining work-life balance is a crucial aspect of our well-being in this fast-paced and demanding world. Achieving a balance between work and personal life can lead to increased productivity, better mental health, and overall satisfaction. Time management plays a key role in this balancing act, as it helps individuals effectively allocate their time between work responsibilities and personal activities. In this comprehensive guide, we will delve deeply into the concept of maintaining work-life balance based on time management principles, explore strategies to achieve this balance, examine the benefits of a harmonious work-life equilibrium, and provide practical examples to illustrate these concepts.

Understanding Work-Life Balance

Work-life balance refers to the equilibrium between the time and effort devoted to work and the time allocated for personal activities, family, leisure, and self-care. It is about prioritizing and managing competing demands to ensure that work commitments do not overpower other facets of life. Achieving work-life balance is essential for both employees and employers, as it leads to enhanced job satisfaction, increased productivity, reduced stress levels, and improved overall well-being.

The Role of Time Management in Work-Life Balance

Time management is the cornerstone of maintaining work-life balance as it involves planning and organizing how time is allocated to various tasks and activities. Effective time management enables individuals to prioritize tasks, set realistic goals, allocate time efficiently, and minimize time-wasting activities. By mastering time management skills, individuals can achieve a better balance between work and personal life, leading to improved mental health, productivity, and overall quality of life.

Strategies for Maintaining Work-Life Balance through Time Management

1. Set Clear Goals and Priorities

Define your short-term and long-term goals both in your professional and personal life. By setting clear priorities, you can focus on tasks that align with your objectives and allocate time accordingly. Use tools like to-do lists, planners, or digital apps to keep track of your goals and priorities.

Example: Sarah, a marketing manager, sets weekly goals for both work-related projects and personal activities. By clearly defining her priorities, she can allocate time effectively to meet her objectives in both realms.

2. Establish Boundaries

Set boundaries between work and personal life to avoid work encroaching on your personal time. Establish specific work hours and stick to them, avoiding work-related tasks during your personal time. Communicate your boundaries to colleagues and supervisors to ensure they respect your personal time.

Example: John sets a rule to avoid checking work emails after 7 p.m. By creating this boundary, he protects his personal time and prevents work-related stress from creeping into his evenings.

3. Delegate Tasks

Delegate tasks at work and home to alleviate your workload and free up time for personal activities. Identify tasks that can be delegated to colleagues, family members, or external services to reduce your burden and create more time for relaxation and self-care.

Example: Maria delegates household chores to her family members to share the responsibility and free up time for hobbies and personal interests. By delegating tasks, she can maintain a healthier work-life balance.

4. Practice Time Blocking

Implement time blocking techniques to allocate specific time slots for different tasks and activities. By segmenting your day into blocks dedicated to work, personal activities, family time, and relaxation, you can ensure that each aspect of your life receives adequate attention.

Example: Tom schedules specific time blocks for work, exercise, family time, and hobbies in his daily calendar. By adhering to the allocated time slots, he maintains a structured routine that balances his professional and personal commitments.

5. Take Regular Breaks

Incorporate regular breaks into your workday to re-energize and prevent burnout. Short breaks between tasks can boost productivity, creativity, and focus. Use break times to engage in activities that help you relax and recharge, such as walking, meditating, or socializing.

Example: Emily takes a 10-minute break every hour to stretch, walk around the office, or enjoy a cup of tea. These short breaks help her stay refreshed and maintain high productivity levels throughout the day.

6. Learn to Say No

Practice saying no to tasks or commitments that do not align with your priorities or overwhelm your schedule. By setting boundaries and declining activities that do not contribute to your well-being, you can protect your time and energy for tasks that matter most.

Example: Peter politely declines additional work projects that would overload his schedule and impact his work-life balance. By learning to say no, he maintains a healthy balance between professional responsibilities and personal life.

7. Maintain a Healthy Lifestyle

Prioritize self-care activities, such as exercise, healthy eating, sleep, and relaxation, to support your overall well-being. A healthy lifestyle plays a vital role in managing stress, boosting energy levels, and enhancing your ability to juggle work and personal commitments effectively.

Example: Anna incorporates regular exercise, nutritious meals, and sufficient sleep into her routine to stay physically and mentally healthy. By prioritizing self-care, she can manage stress and maintain a balanced approach to work and personal life.

Benefits of Maintaining Work-Life Balance through Time Management

1. Improved Productivity

Balancing work and personal life through effective time management enhances productivity by allowing individuals to focus on tasks without distractions and fatigue. By optimizing time allocation and prioritizing tasks, employees can accomplish more in less time, resulting in increased efficiency and performance.

2. Reduced Stress Levels

Maintaining work-life balance through time management helps reduce stress levels by preventing burnout and overload. By setting boundaries, delegating tasks, and taking breaks, individuals can manage their workload effectively and prevent work-related stress from spilling over into personal life.

3. Enhanced Well-Being

A harmonious work-life balance contributes to improved mental health, physical well-being, and overall quality of life. By creating time for personal activities, hobbies, family, and self-care, individuals can nurture their well-being and find fulfillment outside of work responsibilities.

4. Better Relationships

Balancing work and personal life fosters better relationships with family, friends, and colleagues. By being present and engaged during personal interactions, individuals can strengthen their connections, build meaningful relationships, and create a supportive network that enhances their overall happiness and satisfaction.

5. Increased Job Satisfaction

Employees who maintain a healthy work-life balance through effective time management are more satisfied with their jobs and experience greater job fulfillment. By achieving a balance between work and personal life, individuals can find meaning, purpose, and satisfaction in both spheres, leading to overall job satisfaction.

Practical Examples of Maintaining Work-Life Balance through Time Management

Example 1: Mark

Mark is a software engineer who values work-life balance and strives to maintain it through effective time management. To achieve this balance, he follows these strategies:

- Setting Clear Goals: Mark sets weekly goals for both work projects and personal activities, ensuring he allocates time efficiently to meet his objectives.
  - Establishing Boundaries: Mark sets boundaries between work and personal time, avoiding work-related tasks during weekends and evenings to focus on relaxation and hobbies.
  - Practicing Time Blocking: Mark segments his day into time blocks for coding tasks, meetings, exercise, and family time to maintain a structured routine.
  - Taking Regular Breaks: Mark takes short breaks throughout the workday to stretch, walk, or meditate, refreshing his mind and preventing burnout.
  - Learning to Say No: Mark politely declines additional work requests that would overload his schedule, protecting his time for priorities that align with his goals.

By implementing these strategies, Mark successfully maintains a healthy work-life balance and enjoys increased productivity, reduced stress levels, and overall well-being.

Example 2: Laura

Laura is a marketing manager who prioritizes self-care and well-being in her quest for work-life balance. To achieve this balance, she incorporates the following techniques:

- Delegating Tasks: Laura delegates marketing campaigns to her team members, freeing up time for personal activities like yoga classes and painting.
- Practicing Time Blocking: Laura schedules time blocks for strategy meetings, creative brainstorming, exercise, and family dinners, ensuring each aspect of her life receives attention.
- Maintaining a Healthy Lifestyle: Laura prioritizes self-care by exercising regularly, preparing nutritious meals, and getting sufficient sleep to support her physical and mental well-being.
- Taking Regular Breaks: Laura takes short breaks during her workday to relax, meditate, or chat with colleagues, rejuvenating her energy and focus for tasks ahead.
- Establishing Boundaries: Laura sets boundaries between work and personal time, avoiding work-related calls and emails during weekends to devote time to family, hobbies, and relaxation.

By incorporating these strategies into her daily routine, Laura manages to strike a balance between her work commitments and personal well-being, leading to increased job satisfaction and overall happiness.

Conclusion

Achieving work-life balance through effective time management is essential for maintaining our physical, mental, and emotional well-being in today's fast-paced world. By prioritizing tasks, setting boundaries, delegating responsibilities, and practicing self-care, individuals can create a harmonious equilibrium between work and personal life that enhances productivity, reduces stress, and fosters overall satisfaction. By implementing strategies such as goal setting, time blocking, and taking regular breaks, individuals can navigate the demands of work while making time for personal activities, family, and self-care. Ultimately, by mastering time management skills and prioritizing work-life balance, individuals can lead fulfilling and healthy lives marked by success, happiness, and well-being.

Work-life balance is not merely a buzzword but a fundamental aspect of a fulfilling and successful life. By understanding the importance of maintaining this balance and integrating time management strategies into our daily routines, we can embark on a journey towards holistic well-being, productivity, and happiness.

10

Improving Efficiency and Productivity

Improving efficiency and productivity is a critical goal for individuals and organizations across various sectors. Efficiency refers to the ability to accomplish tasks with minimal wasted time, effort, or resources, while productivity is the measure of output produced per unit of input. By enhancing efficiency and productivity, businesses can streamline operations, reduce costs, increase output, and ultimately achieve higher levels of success.

There are several key strategies and best practices that can be implemented to improve efficiency and productivity in various settings. These include optimizing processes, leveraging technology, setting clear goals, fostering a positive work environment, providing adequate training, and continuous monitoring and evaluation. Let's delve deeper into each of these aspects with examples to understand how they can contribute to enhanced efficiency and productivity.

Optimizing Processes:

Optimizing processes is fundamental to improving efficiency and productivity. This involves streamlining workflows, identifying bottlenecks, and eliminating unnecessary steps to ensure that tasks are completed in the most effective and efficient manner. Businesses often use process mapping and analysis techniques such as value stream mapping to identify areas for improvement.

Example: A manufacturing company conducts a value stream mapping exercise to assess its production process. By analyzing each step in the workflow, the company identifies inefficiencies in material handling and transportation. By redesigning the layout of the production floor and implementing a more efficient material flow system, the company reduces lead times and increases productivity.

Leveraging Technology:

Technology plays a crucial role in enhancing efficiency and productivity. Automation, data analytics, and digital tools can streamline tasks, improve accuracy, and enable real-time monitoring of performance metrics. By investing in the right technology solutions, businesses can optimize operations and drive productivity gains.

Example: A retail business implements a cloud-based inventory management system that automatically tracks stock levels, generates purchase orders, and forecasts demand based on historical sales data. By leveraging real-time analytics and automation, the business minimizes stockouts, reduces excess inventory, and improves overall operational efficiency.

Setting Clear Goals:

Setting clear, measurable goals is essential for driving efficiency and productivity. By defining specific targets and objectives, individuals and teams have a clear roadmap to follow and can track their progress towards achieving desired outcomes. Goal alignment across the organization ensures that everyone is working towards a common purpose.

Example: A project manager establishes SMART (Specific, Measurable, Achievable, Relevant, Time-bound) goals for a software development team working on a new product launch. By setting clear milestones for each development phase, providing regular feedback, and monitoring progress against key performance indicators (KPIs), the team stays focused and motivated, leading to improved productivity.

Fostering a Positive Work Environment:

A positive work environment is conducive to improved efficiency and productivity. Factors such as open communication, collaboration, recognition of achievements, and work-life balance can boost employee morale, engagement, and satisfaction. When employees feel valued and supported, they are more likely to perform at their best.

Example: A tech startup emphasizes a culture of trust and empowerment, where employees are encouraged to share ideas, collaborate on projects, and take ownership of their work. By fostering a supportive and inclusive work environment, the company promotes creativity, innovation, and teamwork, leading to higher levels of productivity and employee retention.

Providing Adequate Training:

Investing in employee training and development is critical for enhancing efficiency and productivity. By equipping staff with the necessary skills, knowledge, and tools to perform their roles effectively, organizations can improve performance standards, reduce errors, and increase job satisfaction. Continuous learning opportunities also enable employees to adapt to changing work environments and technologies.

Example: A customer service department conducts regular training sessions on effective communication, problem-solving techniques, and product knowledge for its frontline staff. By providing ongoing training and coaching, the department enhances service quality, resolves customer issues more efficiently, and ultimately improves productivity metrics such as first-call resolution rates and customer satisfaction scores.

Continuous Monitoring and Evaluation:

Continuous monitoring and evaluation of performance metrics are essential for driving efficiency and productivity improvements. By collecting and analyzing data on key performance indicators (KPIs), organizations can identify trends, measure progress towards goals, and pinpoint areas for optimization. Regular performance reviews and feedback mechanisms enable teams to make data-driven decisions and course corrections as needed.

Example: A sales team regularly monitors KPIs such as lead conversion rates, sales pipeline velocity, and customer acquisition costs to assess the effectiveness of their sales strategy. By analyzing performance data, identifying trends, and conducting regular sales reviews, the team can adjust their approach, prioritize high-value leads, and improve overall sales productivity.

In conclusion, improving efficiency and productivity is a multifaceted process that involves optimizing processes, leveraging technology, setting clear goals, fostering a positive work environment, providing adequate training, and continuous monitoring and evaluation. By implementing these strategies and best practices, individuals and organizations can streamline operations, drive performance improvements, and achieve sustainable growth in today's competitive business landscape.

11

Time Management for Specific Situations

Time management is a crucial skill that impacts various aspects of our lives, from personal to professional. Different situations call for specific strategies and approaches to effectively manage time and increase productivity. In this discussion, we will explore time management techniques tailored to specific groups, such as students, professionals, and entrepreneurs.

Students

For students, effective time management is essential to balance academic demands, extracurricular activities, and personal commitments. Here are some strategies students can adopt to improve their time management skills:

1. Prioritize Tasks: Create a to-do list and prioritize tasks based on deadlines and importance. Focus on completing high-priority tasks first to avoid last-minute stress.

2. Set SMART Goals: Set Specific, Measurable, Achievable,

Relevant, and Time-bound (SMART) goals to stay motivated and track progress. Break down larger tasks into smaller, manageable chunks.

3. Create a Schedule: Develop a weekly or daily schedule outlining study blocks, class timings, and extracurricular activities. Allocate specific time slots for each task to maintain a structured routine.

4. Limit Distractions: Identify common distractions like social media, TV, or noisy environments, and eliminate or minimize them during study hours. Use productivity tools like website blockers to stay focused.

5. Take Breaks: Schedule short breaks between study sessions to avoid burnout and enhance productivity. Use techniques like the Pomodoro method (25-minute work intervals followed by a short break) to maintain focus.

6. Utilize Technology: Use tools like calendar apps, task management apps, and online resources for efficient time planning and organization. Set reminders for upcoming deadlines and appointments.

7. Seek Help When Needed: Don't hesitate to seek help from teachers, tutors, or classmates when struggling with a particular subject or assignment. Asking for help can save time and improve understanding.

8. Review and Reflect: Regularly review your progress, assess what worked well, and identify areas for improvement. Reflect

on your time management strategies to make necessary adjustments.

Professionals

Professionals often juggle multiple responsibilities, tasks, and deadlines in a fast-paced work environment. Effective time management is crucial for maintaining productivity and achieving career goals. Here are some time management tips for professionals:

1. Set Clear Goals: Define short-term and long-term goals that align with your professional objectives. Break down goals into actionable steps to track progress and stay focused.

2. Prioritize Tasks: Use techniques like the Eisenhower Matrix to categorize tasks based on urgency and importance. Focus on completing high-priority tasks that contribute to your professional growth.

3. Organize Your Workspace: Maintain a clutter-free and organized workspace to enhance focus and productivity. Keep essential tools and resources within reach to avoid unnecessary distractions.

4. Delegate When Possible: Delegate tasks that can be handled by others to free up time for high-impact projects. Trust your team members and empower them to take ownership of tasks.

5. Establish a Routine: Develop a daily routine that includes dedicated time blocks for specific tasks, meetings, and breaks. Stick to your schedule to build consistency and improve time

management skills.

6. Avoid Multitasking: Focus on one task at a time to maintain quality and efficiency. Multitasking can lead to decreased productivity and increased errors. Complete tasks sequentially to stay on track.

7. Use Time-Blocking Technique: Allocate time blocks for focused work, meetings, email correspondence, and personal development. Schedule uninterrupted work periods to tackle complex tasks efficiently.

8. Learn to Say No: Set boundaries and learn to decline non-essential tasks or commitments that may derail your priorities. Saying no allows you to focus on tasks that align with your professional goals.

9. Continuously Learn and Improve: Stay updated on industry trends, technologies, and best practices to enhance your skills and efficiency. Invest in professional development opportunities to boost your expertise.

Entrepreneurs

Entrepreneurs face unique challenges such as managing business operations, fostering innovation, and balancing personal life. Effective time management is critical for entrepreneurial success. Here are some time management strategies for entrepreneurs:

1. Identify Key Priorities: Determine the most critical tasks that contribute to business growth and success. Focus on activities

that align with your long-term vision and goals.

2. Create a Strategic Plan: Develop a business plan outlining short-term and long-term objectives, strategies, and action plans. Break down goals into specific tasks with deadlines to track progress.

3. Delegate Responsibilities: Delegate tasks that can be handled by employees or freelancers to free up your time for strategic decision-making and business development. Trust your team to execute tasks efficiently.

4. Embrace Technology: Use project management tools, communication platforms, and automation software to streamline business processes and collaboration. Leverage technology to enhance productivity and efficiency.

5. Practice Effective Communication: Clearly communicate expectations, deadlines, and project requirements to team members and stakeholders. Encourage open dialogue and feedback to foster a collaborative work environment.

6. Strive for Work-Life Balance: Prioritize self-care, relaxation, and personal time to prevent burnout and maintain overall well-being. Find a balance between work commitments and personal life to sustain long-term productivity.

7. Stay Flexible and Adaptive: Be prepared to adapt to changing market conditions, customer needs, and industry trends. Embrace innovation and flexibility in your approach to business management and decision-making.

8. Networking and Collaboration: Build a strong professional network of mentors, advisors, and industry contacts to gain insights, support, and opportunities. Collaborate with other entrepreneurs for mutual learning and growth.

In conclusion, effective time management is essential for success in various aspects of life, including academic, professional, and entrepreneurial pursuits. By adopting suitable time management strategies tailored to specific situations, individuals can enhance productivity, achieve goals, and maintain a healthy work-life balance. Continual practice, self-reflection, and adaptation are key to mastering time management skills and maximizing efficiency in both personal and professional endeavors.

12

Monitoring and Adjusting Your Time Management System

Monitoring and adjusting your time management system is a crucial aspect of personal and professional success. Effective time management involves planning, prioritizing, and executing tasks efficiently to achieve goals and maximize productivity. However, simply creating a time management system is not enough; it is equally important to monitor your progress and make necessary adjustments to ensure that you are using your time effectively and making the most of your resources.

In this comprehensive guide, we will explore the importance of monitoring and adjusting your time management system, discuss various strategies for monitoring your time, and provide practical tips on how to make adjustments to improve your time management skills. We will also examine the benefits of effective time management, common challenges that individuals face when managing their time, and how monitoring and adjusting your time management system can help you overcome these challenges.

Why Monitoring and Adjusting Your Time Management System is Important

Effective time management is essential for achieving your goals, increasing productivity, reducing stress, and improving work-life balance. However, even the most well-designed time management system can become less effective over time if it is not monitored and adjusted regularly. Here are some key reasons why monitoring and adjusting your time management system is important:

1. Identifying Inefficiencies: Monitoring your time allows you to identify inefficiencies in your current time management system. By tracking how you spend your time, you can pinpoint areas where you are wasting time or not using your resources effectively.

2. Improving Productivity: Regular monitoring helps you evaluate your progress towards your goals and assess whether you are being productive. By identifying what is working well and what needs improvement, you can make adjustments to enhance your productivity.

3. Adapting to Changes: Circumstances change, and priorities shift. Monitoring your time management system enables you to adapt to new challenges, opportunities, and changes in your schedule. By making adjustments as needed, you can stay on track and maintain productivity.

4. Maintaining Motivation: Seeing progress and accomplishments can boost your motivation and drive to achieve your goals.

MONITORING AND ADJUSTING YOUR TIME MANAGEMENT SYSTEM

By monitoring your time management system and making adjustments to improve efficiency, you can stay motivated and focused on your objectives.

5. Avoiding Burnout: Overloading yourself with tasks or working inefficiently can lead to burnout and decreased performance. Monitoring your time management system helps you identify when you are taking on too much or not managing your time effectively, allowing you to make changes to prevent burnout.

Examples of Monitoring and Adjusting Your Time Management System

To better understand how monitoring and adjusting your time management system works in practice, let's consider a few examples:

1. Example 1: Daily Time Tracking

Sarah, a marketing manager, wants to improve her time management skills to meet project deadlines more effectively. She starts by tracking her daily activities using a time tracking app. After a week of monitoring her time, Sarah notices that she spends an excessive amount of time in meetings and on administrative tasks. To adjust her time management system, she decides to limit the duration of meetings and delegate some administrative tasks to team members. By making these adjustments, Sarah is able to allocate more time to high-priority tasks and improve her overall productivity.

2. Example 2: Weekly Review and Planning

John, a freelance writer, struggles to balance his work with personal commitments. To enhance his time management, he sets aside time each Sunday for a weekly review and planning session. During this session, John reviews his previous week's activities, identifies areas where he fell short, and plans his upcoming week's tasks and priorities. By regularly reviewing and adjusting his time management system, John is able to stay organized, meet deadlines, and maintain a healthy work-life balance.

3. Example 3: Quarterly Goal Evaluation

Michael, a project manager, sets quarterly goals for his team to achieve project milestones and deliverables. At the end of each quarter, Michael conducts a goal evaluation session to review the team's progress, assess what went well and where improvements are needed, and adjust their strategies for the next quarter. By monitoring their performance regularly and making adjustments based on past successes and challenges, Michael's team improves their efficiency and effectiveness in achieving project goals.

Strategies for Monitoring Your Time

Monitoring your time effectively requires adopting strategies and tools that help you track and analyze how you spend your time. Here are some popular strategies for monitoring your time:

1. Time Tracking Apps: Use time tracking apps or software tools to monitor your daily activities, track how much time you spend

on tasks, and identify patterns in your time usage. Popular time tracking apps include Toggl, RescueTime, and Clockify.

2. Activity Logs: Keep a detailed log of your daily activities, including work-related tasks, personal commitments, and leisure activities. Reviewing your activity log regularly can help you identify time-wasting activities and areas where you can improve your time management.

3. Pomodoro Technique: Practice the Pomodoro Technique, which involves working in short, focused intervals (typically 25 minutes) followed by a short break. By tracking your work periods and breaks, you can assess your productivity levels and make adjustments to optimize your work sessions.

4. Time Audits: Conduct periodic time audits where you analyze how you spent your time over a specific period (e.g., a week or a month). Reflect on your accomplishments, challenges, and areas for improvement to identify ways to enhance your time management skills.

5. Goal Setting and Tracking: Set specific goals for your tasks and projects and track your progress towards achieving them. By monitoring your goal progress, you can ensure that you are working towards your objectives effectively and adjust your strategies as needed.

Practical Tips for Adjusting Your Time Management System

Once you have monitored your time and identified areas for improvement, it is essential to make adjustments to your time management system to enhance your productivity and effectiveness. Here are some practical tips for adjusting your time management system:

1. Prioritize Tasks: Identify your high-priority tasks and allocate more time to tasks that contribute significantly to your goals. Adjust your schedule to focus on critical tasks first before moving on to less important activities.

2. Delegate Tasks: If you find yourself overwhelmed with tasks, consider delegating some of them to team members, colleagues, or outsourcing services. Delegate tasks that others can do more efficiently to free up your time for tasks that require your expertise.

3. Eliminate Time-Wasting Activities: Identify activities that do not contribute to your goals or consume excessive time without providing significant value. Eliminate or minimize these time-wasting activities to free up more time for important tasks.

4. Batch Similar Tasks: Group similar tasks together and work on them in batches to maximize efficiency and reduce task-switching time. By focusing on similar tasks at once, you can streamline your workflow and complete tasks more quickly.

5. Set Boundaries: Establish boundaries to protect your time and energy. Learn to say no to tasks that do not align with your priorities or goals and set clear work hours to avoid overworking and burnout.

6. Regularly Review and Adjust: Schedule regular time to

review your time management system, assess your progress, and make necessary adjustments. Reflect on what worked well and what needs improvement to continuously enhance your time management skills.

Benefits of Effective Time Management

Effective time management offers numerous benefits that can positively impact your personal and professional life. Here are some key benefits of mastering time management:

1. Increased Productivity: Effective time management helps you complete tasks more efficiently, reduce procrastination, and increase your overall productivity.

2. Improved Focus and Concentration: By prioritizing tasks and minimizing distractions, you can improve your focus and concentration, leading to better performance and outcomes.

3. Better Work-Life Balance: Properly managing your time allows you to allocate time for work, personal activities, hobbies, and relaxation, leading to a balanced and fulfilling lifestyle.

4. Reduced Stress and Anxiety: Organizing your tasks and following a structured schedule can reduce stress and anxiety associated with deadlines and overwhelming workloads.

5. Enhanced Goal Achievement: Efficient time management enables you to work towards your goals systematically, track your progress, and achieve desired outcomes in a timely manner.

6. Increased Opportunities for Growth: By managing your time effectively, you create space for learning new skills, pursuing personal development opportunities, and exploring new avenues for growth and advancement.

Common Time Management Challenges

Despite the benefits of effective time management, many individuals face common challenges that hinder their ability to manage their time efficiently. Some of the common time management challenges include:

1. Procrastination: Putting off tasks or delaying important activities can lead to missed deadlines, increased stress, and reduced productivity.

2. Lack of Prioritization: Failing to prioritize tasks effectively can result in spending time on low-impact activities while neglecting important tasks.

3. Time Wasting Activities: Engaging in activities that do not contribute to your goals or waste time can reduce your overall productivity and effectiveness.

4. Overcommitment: Taking on too many tasks or commitments can lead to overburdening yourself, resulting in burnout, decreased quality of work, and missed deadlines.

5. Task Switching: Constantly switching between tasks can reduce your efficiency and focus, leading to longer completion times and lower quality output.

How Monitoring and Adjusting Your Time Management System Can Help

To address these common time management challenges and improve your overall efficiency, monitoring and adjusting your time management system plays a crucial role. Here is how monitoring and adjusting your time management system can help you overcome these challenges:

1. Identifying Inefficiencies: By monitoring your time, you can identify time-wasting activities, prioritize tasks effectively, and eliminate inefficiencies that hinder your productivity.

2. Optimizing Task Allocation: Regular monitoring allows you to track your progress on tasks, adjust priorities as needed, and allocate time more efficiently to high-impact activities.

3. Enhancing Focus and Productivity: Adjusting your time management system based on your performance and progress helps you stay focused, reduce distractions, and improve your overall productivity.

4. Preventing Burnout: Monitoring your workload and adjusting your schedule to manage your time effectively can help prevent burnout caused by overcommitment and excessive workload.

5. Improving Goal Achievement: By tracking your progress towards goals, adjusting your strategies, and making necessary improvements, you can enhance your chances of achieving your objectives within the desired timeframe.

Conclusion

Monitoring and adjusting your time management system is a continuous process that requires reflection, evaluation, and adaptation. By tracking how you spend your time, identifying inefficiencies, and making necessary adjustments, you can enhance your productivity, achieve your goals, and maintain a healthy work-life balance.

Effective time management is not a one-size-fits-all approach; it requires experimentation, learning from experience, and continuous improvement. By incorporating monitoring and adjustment strategies into your time management system, you can overcome common time management challenges, increase your productivity, and create opportunities for personal and professional growth.

Remember that effective time management is a skill that can be honed over time through practice, self-awareness, and a willingness to adapt to changing circumstances. By taking proactive steps to monitor and adjust your time management system, you can optimize your use of time, improve your efficiency, and achieve greater success in all aspects of your life.

www.ingramcontent.com/pod-product-compliance
Lightning Source LLC
Chambersburg PA
CBHW071214240526
45470CB00018B/1864